Mixtures and Solutions

Hugh Westrup

Consultant

Trent Nash, M.S.E.
Aerospace Engineer

Publishing Credits

Rachelle Cracchiolo, M.S.Ed., *Publisher*
Conni Medina, M.A.Ed., *Managing Editor*
Diana Kenney, M.A.Ed., NBCT, *Content Director*
Dona Herweck Rice, *Series Developer*
Robin Erickson, *Multimedia Designer*
Timothy Bradley, *Illustrator*

Image Credits: p.4 Mike Clarke/iStock; p.6 (left) Dirk Wiersma/Science Source, (right) iStock; p7 (background, bottom left) iStock; p.9 GIPhotoStock/Science Source; p.10 (sidebar) iStock; p13. (top, bottom right) iStock; p.16 Photo Researchers; p.18 Phil Degginger/Science Source p.20 Martyn F. Chillmaid/Science Source; p.22 Richard Hutchings/Science Source; p.23 Phil Degginger/Science Source; p.24-25 Charles D. Winters/Science Source; p. 25 Charles D. Winters/Science Source; p.28-29 (illustrations) Timothy Bradley; all other images from Shutterstock.

Library of Congress Cataloging-in-Publication Data

Westrup, Hugh, author.
Mixtures and solutions / Hugh Westrup.
pages cm
Summary: "When you mix chocolate and milk together you're making a mixture. Oatmeal cookies are mixtures, too. But chocolate milk and cookies are different kinds of mixtures. How many different types of cookies can you think of? You already know more about chemistry than you thought!"-- Provided by publisher.
Audience: Grades 4 to 6
Includes index.
ISBN 978-1-4807-4721-0 (pbk.)
1. Solution (Chemistry)--Juvenile literature.
2. Emulsions--Juvenile literature.
3. Chemistry--Juvenile literature. I. Title.
QD541.W435 2016
541.34--dc23

2015003158

Teacher Created Materials

5301 Oceanus Drive
Huntington Beach, CA 92649-1030
http://www.tcmpub.com

ISBN 978-1-4807-4721-0

Table of Contents

Itty-Bitty Bits

What's the smallest thing you can think of? Now, take a hammer and smash it in your mind. What makes up the smaller pieces?

All matter, whether it's smaller than a grain of sand or as big as a whale, is made up of itty-bitty bits called **atoms**. Atoms are too small to see with the human eye or even most microscopes. Atoms combine to create **molecules**. Molecules combine to create everything we see in the universe.

Water without any minerals is called *distilled water*. Most people don't like the way it tastes because we're used to the taste of minerals.

This machine crushes rocks to itty-bitty bits.

Molecules and atoms can take the form of a solid, a liquid, or a gas. Each state of matter has its own properties. Solids can be hard or soft. Plastic, metal, stone, bone, straw, sand, and feathers are all solids. Objects in a solid state don't change size or shape unless they are cut or broken.

Unlike solids, liquids change shape. They can flow, pour, and even spill. They change their shape to fill the space around them. Milk, oil, and ink are all liquids.

Gases don't have any shape or size of their own. They spread freely to fill the space around them. Similar to liquids, gases flow easily. But they can also be **compressed**, or squeezed. Gases are often invisible. So most of the time, we can't see them. But gases are all around us.

Together, these three states of matter make up most everything in the universe.

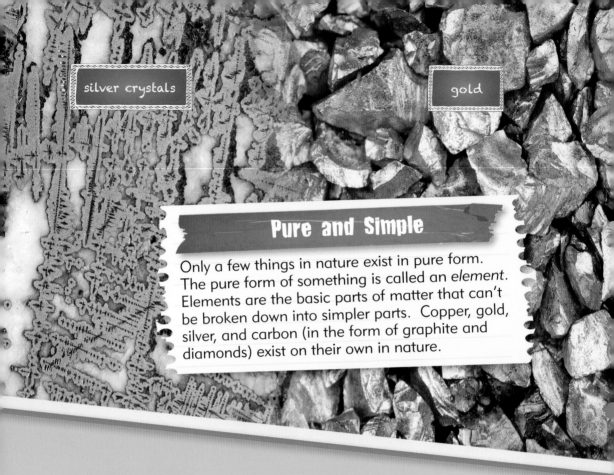

silver crystals

gold

Pure and Simple

Only a few things in nature exist in pure form. The pure form of something is called an *element*. Elements are the basic parts of matter that can't be broken down into simpler parts. Copper, gold, silver, and carbon (in the form of graphite and diamonds) exist on their own in nature.

All Mixed Up

The world would get pretty boring if each **substance** could only be found on its own. But substances combine to form **mixtures**. There are mixtures everywhere in the world—millions of them. Air is a mixture of gases. Rocks are mixtures of minerals. Oceans and lakes are mixtures of gases, minerals, and water.

Most of the things we eat are mixtures. Think about a salad. It's a mixture. The tomatoes are still tomatoes. The lettuce is still lettuce. The carrots are still carrots. But together they make a nutritious—and tasty—mixture. The wide variety of mixtures in our food is what creates so many different flavors. And if a meal wasn't a mixture when it entered your mouth, it is by the time it leaves your stomach!

carbon

Smoke, blood, and water are all mixtures.

Water is a mixture of pure water and minerals.

Smoke is a mixture of chemical particles in the air.

Blood is a mixture of plasma, red blood cells, white blood cells, and platelets.

The different parts of a mixture mingle loosely. That makes it possible to separate them from one another. You can pick out the various ingredients in a salad with a fork. Other mixtures might require a more precise tool to pick them apart. You might need a magnet or filter paper to do the job. But when you separate a mixture, you can find the original substances you started with.

Mixtures can be sorted into two categories, with few exceptions. **Heterogeneous mixtures** are made of substances you can see. Vegetable soup is a heterogeneous mixture. So is trail mix.

The substances in **homogeneous mixtures** have been mixed together thoroughly and are spread evenly throughout. If you examine a piece of the mixture, it will look just like any other piece of the mixture, no matter how small the sample. Milk is a homogeneous mixture. It contains protein, sugar, water, and fat, but these substances cannot easily be separated or tasted individually. Regardless of how you pour it, each glass of milk looks the same.

Can't remember the difference between heterogeneous and homogeneous? Look to the root words. *Hetero* means "different" and *homo* means "the same."

Smoothies

A smoothie is a heterogeneous mixture. The fruit or vegetables, ice, and juice can separate over time.

Heterogeneous Mixtures

Suspensions are one of the most common types of heterogeneous mixtures. One part of a suspension is always liquid. The other part is a solid or a liquid. One substance always settles to the bottom of the container. Suspensions change and separate over time.

Most salad dressings are suspensions. They usually contain oil and vinegar, which don't mix. That's why salad dressing labels say, "Shake well before using." Liquid medicines often have the same directions.

Paints are also suspensions. They contain a solid pigment, or color, and a liquid. If a can of paint has been sitting on the shelf for a while, the pigment sinks to the bottom. Before the can of paint is sold, it's placed in a machine that shakes it. That motion stirs the paint so the pigment and the liquid are thoroughly combined again. If you don't mix **solutions** well, you'll quickly notice the results!

A Clear Sign

Suspensions are never completely clear. They're usually murky. After sitting for a while, suspensions will have a distinct line where the substances start to separate.

chalk and water

suspension immediately after stirring

suspension after being left to sit

Homogeneous Mixtures

It's easy to create a homogeneous mixture. Just pour a teaspoon of salt in a glass of water and stir. Watch the salt disappear in the water. The result is another type of mixture: a solution. A solution is a homogeneous mixture in which the separate parts can't be seen without a microscope.

A solution has two parts. The first part is the **solute**. The solute is the part that's dissolved. In saltwater, salt is the solute. The other part is the **solvent**. It's the part that does the dissolving. In saltwater, water is the solvent. You can't see the solute in a solution, which is why you can't see the salt in saltwater.

atoms in a crystal of salt

Types of Solutions

A solution can take many forms.

Liquid Dissolved in Liquid

Vinegar is acetic acid dissolved in water.

Gases Dissolved in Gases

The air we breathe is oxygen and carbon dioxide dissolved in nitrogen.

Solids Dissolved in Solids

Steel is carbon dissolved in iron.

salt

Solutions can be made of solids, liquids, or gases. You can dissolve solids in liquids. You can also dissolve liquids and gases in liquids. Soft drinks are carbon dioxide gas dissolved in water and liquid flavoring. (The bubbles you see are really the carbon dioxide coming out of the solution. Who knew a solution could taste so good!) Gases are often dissolved in gases. A solid can even be dissolved in a solid.

Look at the label on your milk. It probably says *homogenized milk.* Most milk is homogenized to prevent the fat in it from separating.

water and salt atoms combining

saltwater

Colloids

In a **colloid**, small particles are scattered evenly throughout a substance. In some ways, a colloid is like a solution. It appears homogeneous. But in other ways, a colloid is like a heterogeneous mixture.

If you shine a light through a solution, the light will pass through in a clean line. But that same light will be scattered when it's shined through a colloid. That's because the particles in a colloid are bigger than those in a solution. They're big enough to block the light.

Colloid particles are still smaller and lighter than the particles in a suspension. In a colloid, one part doesn't settle to the bottom the way it does in a suspension. It remains suspended and spread throughout the mixture.

solution

colloid

The cells in your body are filled with *colloids!*

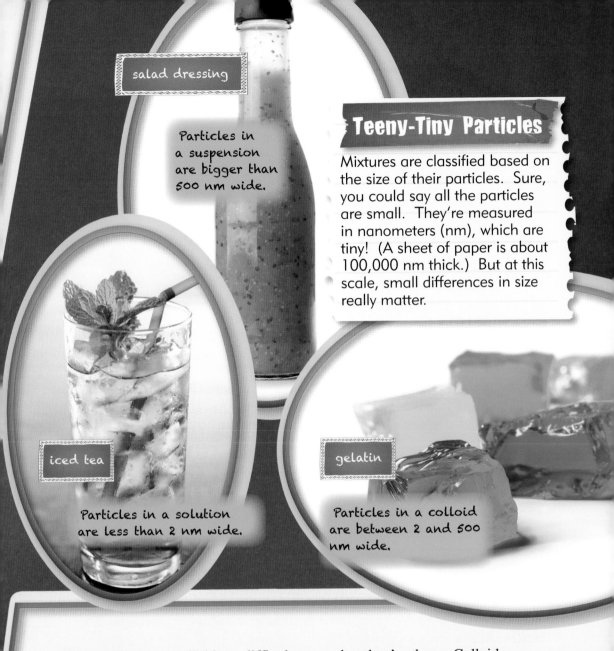

salad dressing

Particles in a suspension are bigger than 500 nm wide.

Teeny-Tiny Particles

Mixtures are classified based on the size of their particles. Sure, you could say all the particles are small. They're measured in nanometers (nm), which are tiny! (A sheet of paper is about 100,000 nm thick.) But at this scale, small differences in size really matter.

iced tea

Particles in a solution are less than 2 nm wide.

gelatin

Particles in a colloid are between 2 and 500 nm wide.

The particles in a colloid are difficult to see, but they're there. Colloid particles might be liquid droplets, gas bubbles, or solid particles. Colloids come in many forms. Fog is a colloid. It's a mixture of tiny water droplets floating evenly in the air. Smoke is a colloid, too. It's made of solid particles of soot, ash, and tar spread evenly throughout the air. They may sound exotic, but colloids can be found in nearly every home. Many products we know and love are colloids. Jams, jellies, mayonnaise, and marshmallows are colloids. Ink, toothpaste, shaving cream, and hand lotion are colloids as well.

A Solution, NOT a Problem

Creating a solution isn't just a way to solve a problem! It's also an important part of chemistry.

Aqueous Solution

Have you ever spilled something such as pasta sauce or chocolate ice cream on your clothes? You probably soaked the item in water to dissolve the stain so it didn't absorb into the fabric. Water is what scientists call a *universal solvent*. That's because it can be used to dissolve many things.

The term *universal solvent* dates back more than 500 years to the Middle Ages. At that time, people practiced alchemy, which is a mix of science, magic, and mythology. Medieval alchemists wanted to find a substance that dissolved everything—a universal solvent. In reality, water can't dissolve everything. But it dissolves more substances than any other solvent. Over the centuries, the name has proven it is well earned.

Why is water such a good solvent? It has **polarity**. Every molecule of water has a negative area and a positive area. Stir a spoonful of sugar into a glass of water. Every sugar molecule has a positive area and a negative area. The negative area of each water molecule is attracted to the positive area of each sugar molecule. And the positive area of each water molecule is attracted to the negative area of each sugar molecule. Those attractions hold the sugar molecules between the water molecules. The result is a solution. And since most solutes are polar, water can dissolve them.

sugar water

sugar

A Slippery Truth

Oil is nonpolar and will only dissolve other nonpolar molecules. And only nonpolar items can dissolve it. That means if you get oil on your clothes, you can't just use water to get it out! Rubbing alcohol or dishwashing liquid works better.

oil spill

Solubility

Not every substance can dissolve other substances. Salt can be dissolved in water. But it can't be dissolved in cooking oil. In other words, salt is soluble in water, but insoluble in cooking oil. Sugar is also soluble in water and insoluble in cooking oil.

Even though salt is soluble in water, only a certain amount will dissolve. Beyond that amount, any more salt will settle to the bottom. The maximum amount of solute that can dissolve in a solvent is the solubility. At room temperature, the most salt you can dissolve in 100 milliliters (mL) of water is 36 grams (g). So its solubility is said to be 36 g/100 mL. You can dissolve 180 g of sugar into 100 mL of water, so it has a higher solubility.

Concentration

Check out the label on a bottle of vinegar. You'll see a percentage printed on it. It might be 5, 6, or 7 percent. That percentage is the vinegar's concentration. Concentration is how much solute is in a solution. Vinegar is a solution of acetic acid (solute) in water (solvent). A 5 percent solution of vinegar contains 5 percent acetic acid and 95 percent water.

DISTILLED WHITE
VINEGAR
EST. 1869 EST.

THE ALL NATURAL
CHOICE FOR FOOD
See Back
5% ACIDITY

See Back

5% ACIDITY

Solubility can change. Heat usually increases solubility. You can dissolve more salt or sugar in hot water than you can in cold water. This happens because the molecules in hot water move faster and farther apart than those in cold water. The solute has more space to expand, so more of it can dissolve. The opposite is true for most gases. Gases tend to be more soluble in cold water than they are in hot water.

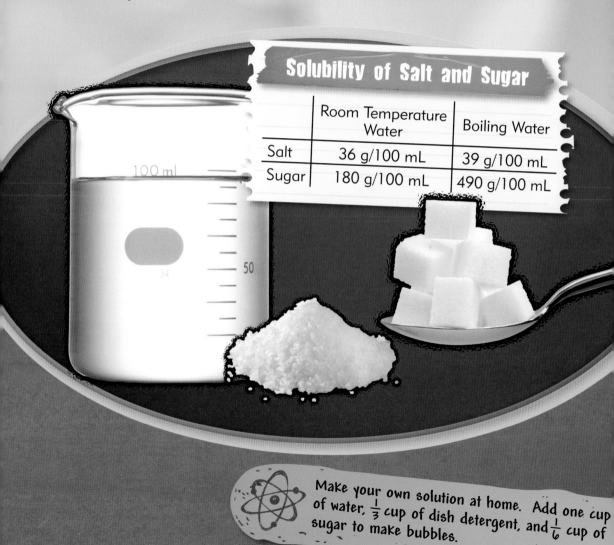

Solubility of Salt and Sugar

	Room Temperature Water	Boiling Water
Salt	36 g/100 mL	39 g/100 mL
Sugar	180 g/100 mL	490 g/100 mL

Make your own solution at home. Add one cup of water, $\frac{1}{3}$ cup of dish detergent, and $\frac{1}{6}$ cup of sugar to make bubbles.

Solutes can have strong effects on solvents. You can see this effect in water. Distilled water is pure. Unlike tap water, it doesn't contain any dissolved minerals. Distilled water won't conduct electricity. But if you dissolve table salt or other minerals in it, it becomes an excellent conductor. That's why you should always dry your hands before handling any electrical devices. And you shouldn't operate electrical devices near sinks or bathtubs.

Solutes can also change the boiling point of a solvent. Distilled water boils at 100° Celsius (212° Fahrenheit). But adding salt to it will make it boil at a higher temperature. The more salt you add to water, the higher the boiling point is.

More or Less

Chemists use different terms to describe solutions depending on how much solute is in them.

A dilute solution contains a small amount of solute.

A concentrated solution contains a large amount of solute.

A saturated solution contains the maximum amount of solute.

Make Room for Changes

When a solvent is by itself, its molecules are able to boil, freeze, and evaporate as normal. But when a solute is added to it, the solute's molecules get in the way of the solvent. The different molecules are busy knocking into each other. That's what changes the boiling point, freezing point, and evaporation process.

When liquid is below the freezing point but is not yet frozen, it is called *supercooled liquid*.

Similarly, solutes can also lower the freezing point of a solvent. Distilled water freezes at 0°C (32°F). Adding salt to the water will lower its freezing point. Roads are salted in cold areas during the winter so that water freezes at lower temperatures.

Finally, a solute can change how quickly something evaporates. Evaporation occurs when a liquid turns into a gas. Place a dish of pure water and a dish of saltwater on a windowsill. The pure water will evaporate faster than the saltwater.

Reversing the Process

A mixture is a substance that results from a **physical change**. A physical change is a change that does not result in a new substance. For example, if you fold a sheet of paper in half, you still have paper—it just looks different.

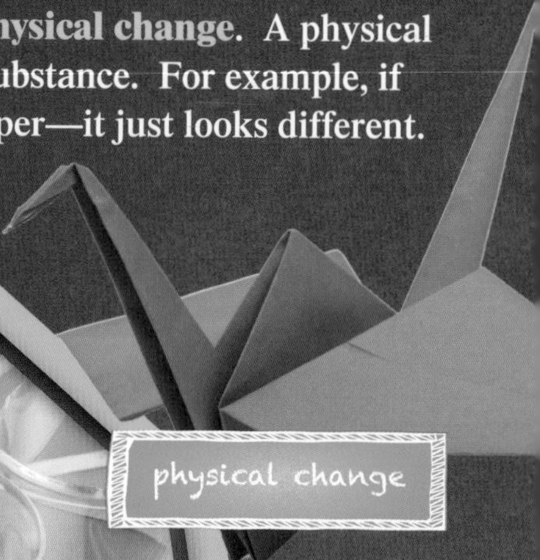

physical change

chemical change

92.95 g

EK-200i

EK-200i

92.95 g

Conserving Mass

Whether it's a suspension, a solution, or a colloid, the types of atoms in the mixture remain the same from start to finish. The number of atoms doesn't change either. This means the **mass** of the mixture equals the combined mass of the original substance.

This is different from a **chemical change**. A chemical change occurs when atoms or molecules of different substances react with one another. They join to form new molecules. A new substance is created. If you burn a sheet of paper, you won't have paper anymore. Instead, you'd have ash, smoke, and water vapor. Unlike physical changes, chemical changes cannot be reversed or undone.

There are usually signs that a chemical change is taking place. If you notice foaming, bubbling, smoke, or fire, then you are probably observing a chemical change. But if you are simply making a mixture, you won't see this. You will not see smoke if you mix chocolate syrup with milk. But keep in mind, not all things are safe to mix together! Always ask an adult before creating mixtures.

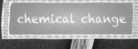

chemical change

Complex Compounds?

People sometimes confuse mixtures with **compounds**. But the two are very different. When a mixture is created, the various parts mingle but still exist separately from one another. When a compound is created, the parts combine to form something new.

Mixture

- physical change used to create mixtures and separate them into substances
- combination of parts can vary
- properties are related to components
- examples include rocks, milk, tap water, and air

Compound

- chemical change used to create compounds and separate them into elements
- combination of parts does not vary
- properties are different from components
- examples include salt, baking soda, pure water, and sugar

Every mixture can be taken apart. Its components will be the same as they were when the mixture was put together. There are several ways to separate a mixture.

Suppose you have a mixture of iron filings and sand. Magnets can separate the two substances. If you run a magnet through the mixture, it will attract the iron filings and remove them from the sand.

Sifting is another simple way to separate two solids from each other. Only the small particles will pass through the metal mesh of a sieve (siv), or sifter. The larger particles will be trapped on top of the sieve.

Filtration can separate a mixture of a solid and a liquid. A filter is paper or cloth with very tiny holes in it. If a solid-liquid mixture is poured onto a filter, the liquid will pass through the holes. But the solid particles will be held back. You can try this by placing mud onto a cloth. The cloth will work like a filter and let the water pass through. The solid particles will stay on top.

Magnetic Attraction

Some breakfast cereals contain bits of iron, which is an essential nutrient for humans. Our bodies need iron to carry oxygen through our bloodstream. Try crushing cereal that contains iron. Then, run a strong magnet through it. The magnet will attract bits of iron.

Gravity can also separate mixtures. For instance, over time, gravity will pull salt downward.

All Shook Up

Agitation is another way to separate some mixtures. You've seen agitation at work when you shake a soft drink. Shaking the can causes the dissolved carbon dioxide to suddenly rise out of the solution. The carbon dioxide gas forces the soft drink to spurt out of the can.

Evaporation is another way to separate solids from liquids in a mixture. If you take a sugar-water solution and leave it in an open container, the water will evaporate into the air. The sugar will be left behind in the container.

Condensation is the opposite of evaporation. Condensation is the change that occurs when a gas turns into a liquid. It, too, can help separate mixtures. Condensation turns the water vapor into liquid water and separates it from air.

Scientists use evaporation and condensation in the process of distillation. First, a solid-liquid solution is poured into a beaker over a high heat. Once the solution boils, the liquid evaporates, leaving the solid in the beaker. Gas then rises into a long glass tube. There, it cools and condenses back into a liquid, which is collected at the end of the tube.

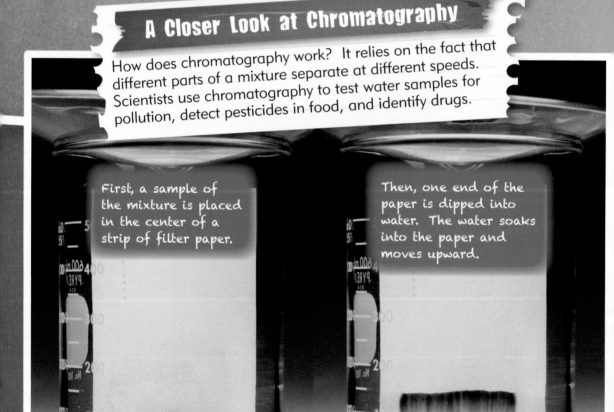

A Closer Look at Chromatography

How does chromatography work? It relies on the fact that different parts of a mixture separate at different speeds. Scientists use chromatography to test water samples for pollution, detect pesticides in food, and identify drugs.

First, a sample of the mixture is placed in the center of a strip of filter paper.

Then, one end of the paper is dipped into water. The water soaks into the paper and moves upward.

A solution of two liquids can also be distilled. As the solution is heated, the liquid with the lower boiling point will change into gas first. The condenser will collect that gas and cool it into a liquid. The other liquid is left behind in the beaker. The distillation process separates individual substances, making a pure substance. For example, saltwater can be distilled, and the result is fresh drinking water.

Chromatography is another way to separate mixtures. It is also one of the most useful. It's fast and simple. It can help you find tiny amounts of a substance in a mixture. And it can help you examine mixtures that have many ingredients.

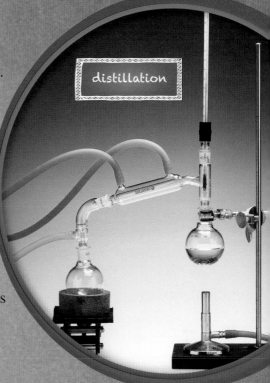

distillation

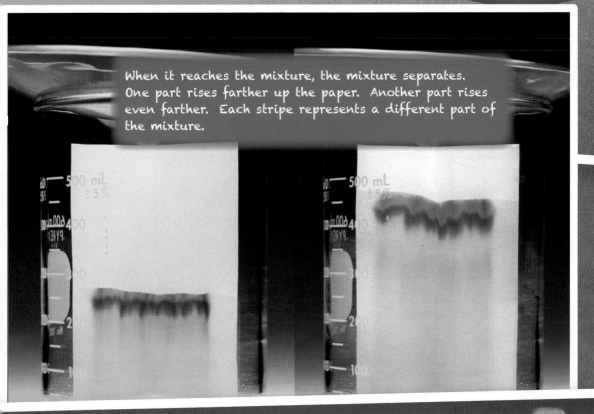

When it reaches the mixture, the mixture separates. One part rises farther up the paper. Another part rises even farther. Each stripe represents a different part of the mixture.

Living in a Mixed-Up World

Why are chemists so great at solving problems? Because they have all the solutions! Get it? Knowing how mixtures and solutions work makes our lives easier. Spill something? Grab some water to dissolve it! Want to see what root beer is made of? Try letting it evaporate and see what you're left with! You can mix, match, and unmix mixtures all day long. And you can always undo whatever you create. That's the beauty of mixtures!

Mixtures and solutions also make our lives more enjoyable. Pizza, oatmeal raisin cookies, smoothies, and lemonade are just a few mixtures and solutions that people enjoy every day.

Look for all the mixtures that surround us in our messy, mixed-up world. See if you can identify heterogeneous mixtures, homogeneous mixtures, and colloids. Then, try making your own! Which combination is your favorite? Record your results and see if you notice any patterns. Once you start, you won't be able to stop.

Trail Mix: Trial and Error

What's the best mixture for trail mix?
You decide. Combine your ingredients,
take a bite, and rate it. Then, separate
the ingredients, and remix them to
make a brand-new creation!

Think Like a Scientist

Which substances are soluble? Experiment and find out!

What to Get

- clear glasses
- hot and cold water
- stopwatch
- substances to dissolve such as sugar, pepper, sand, and hot chocolate powder
- teaspoon

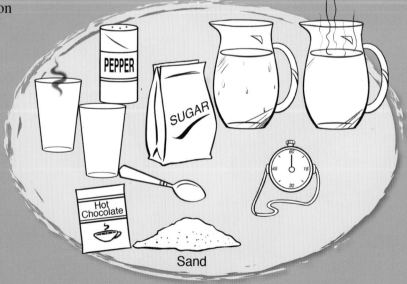

What to Do

1 Fill a glass with hot water and a glass with cold water. Add a teaspoon of sugar to each cup and stir.

2 Use a stopwatch to keep track of time. Stir the water gently for 10 seconds. On a chart like the one below, record what the mixtures look like. After 60 seconds, record the results again.

3 Repeat the experiment again in fresh water using different solutes such as pepper, sand, and hot chocolate. Be sure to rinse the glasses each time.

	Hot Water	Cold Water
Sugar after 10 seconds of stirring		
Sugar 60 seconds later		

Glossary

ns—the smallest particles of
a substance that can exist by
hemselves

mical change—a change that
results in a new substance

oid—a very finely divided
substance is scattered throughout
another substance

pounds—substances made
of two or more types of atoms
bonded together

pressed—pressed together

erogeneous mixtures—mixtures
n which the parts are not evenly
mixed or completely spread out

ogeneous mixtures—mixtures
n which parts are evenly mixed
and completely spread out

s—the amount of matter an
object contains

tures—two or more components
that are combined but keep their
own properties

ecules—the smallest possible
amounts of particular substances
that have all the characteristics of
those substances

physical change—a change that does
not form a new substance

polarity—the condition of having
positive and negative charges and
especially magnetic or electrical
poles

solubility—a measure of how much
solute can be dissolved in a
specific solvent

soluble—capable of being dissolved

solute—a substance that is dissolved
in another substance

solutions—liquids in which things
have been dissolved

solvent—a substance in which
something can be dissolved

substance—a material of a particular
kind

suspensions—substances (usually
a liquid) that have very small
pieces of a solid material mixed
throughout them

Index

YOUR TURN!

Food for Thought

Celebrate the mixtures all around you with a party! Grab some friends and cook up a solution and a colloid to chow down on. Don't forget to make a heterogeneous mixture (How about a pizza?) and a suspension (How about some salad dressing?). Observe how each item is different. Observe how each is similar. Talk about the mixtures with your friends. At this party, there's bound to be something for everyone!